Edward Isidore Sears

The Central Park under Ring-Leader Rule

Edward Isidore Sears

The Central Park under Ring-Leader Rule

ISBN/EAN: 9783337159573

Printed in Europe, USA, Canada, Australia, Japan

Cover: Foto ©ninafisch / pixelio.de

More available books at **www.hansebooks.com**

UNDER RING-LEADER RULE.

REPRINTED FROM THE

NATIONAL QUARTERLY REVIEW,

(No. XLIV., March, 1871,)

Edited by EDW. I. SEARS, LL.D.

NEW YORK:

EDWARD I. SEARS,

658 BROADWAY.

1871.

NOTE TO THE READER.

It is but justice to the great Tammany naturalist to admit that so great is the confidence of the public in his profound and learned researches, especially in the *vegetable* kingdom, that the very imperfect sketch we have given of his " works " has pretty nearly exhausted even the edition of the *Review* which we announced as affording a " full supply."

But its due weight should be given to the fact that the *étude* has had the honor of being recommended in a letter to the *Herald*—and published as an advertisement in other journals—even by so high an authority as his Serene Highness the Doge of New York, and ex-Know-Nothing chieftain,* than whom no one is more fully acquainted with the enviable merits of that famous *savant*.

True, other sketches by the *Quarterly* Editor have been similarly recommended by quack doctors, insurance quacks, quack pedagogues, Bowery and " Black Crook " dramatists, poetasters, *et hoc genus omne;* several having kindly put themselves to the trouble and expense of issuing large pamphlets for his benefit : but he confesses, with due gratitude, that the greatest honor yet conferred on him is that of his Serene Highness, the renowned Know-Nothing Doge, and Protector-in-chief of the Irish, in his very appropriate and admirably sustained rôle as the *miles gloriosus* (Anglice *bully*), of our great Tammany naturalist.

Journals like the *Transcript* (Chambers street), are authorised to insert this notice three times (provided the total cost does not exceed one dollar), and send bill to Dr. Sears, *National Quarterly* Office, who can say, without fear of contradiction, that although he has never had or sought any fat jobs to profit by at the expense of his fellow-citizens, he has never defrauded printer or anybody else of as much as half-a-dollar.

In order to place the great result accomplished at the Central Park within the reach of all who are interested in parks, gardens, quack medicines, coaches-and-six, etc., etc., only 25 cents will be charged for the pamphlet.

* See letter of thanks to that illustrious personage in the *Herald* of April 7, 1871.

THE
CENTRAL PARK UNDER RING-LEADER RULE.

WHEN Gustavus III. requested the great Linnæus to give him some hints for his new park on the banks of the Dahl, the philosopher sent him the following, among others: "Your majesty should commit your favorite horses to the care of an ignorant groom, or place your choice cattle in charge of an ignorant cow-boy, rather than entrust your trees and shrubs to the manipulations of an ignorant gardener. But, above all the candidates for the supervision of your park, *beware of petty politicians.*"*

To many this may seem to exagerate the importance of selecting for the management of parks and gardens only those whose intelligence, tastes, and habits qualify them, at least to some extent, for the duties which they are expected to perform. But we think that all willing to be convinced, who will favor us with their attention for one hour, or even half an hour, will admit that the philosopher was right. Although we pretend to have gleaned some knowledge of botany—having spent more than one decade among trees, and shrubs, and plants, not altogether unmindful of the phenomena they present under certain circumstances—we shall not ask the reader to accept our views as to what may be expected from the present "supervision" of the Central Park further than we shall be found able to sustain them by those of men whose authority cannot be disputed.

* *Collectio Epistolarum quas ad viros illustres et clarissimos scripsit Carolus a Linne.* (Collection of Letters written to illustrious and celebrated men, etc.)

The main facts require, indeed, no elaborate testimony; they can be judged without any extensive knowledge of botany or any other science. Common sense and ordinary intelligence, with a moderate use of one's eyes, are sufficient qualifications for the task. We should be very stupid if we did not know something, not only of the manner in which the Park is managed, but also of the results and general tendency of its management; for none have visited it more frequently, or more regularly, at all seasons, during the last ten years, than we. Not content with riding or driving whithersoever a horse may go, there is not a pedestrian walk with whose attractions we are not familiar. That we do not make our almost daily visits in any fault-finding spirit, however, may be inferred from the fact that this is our first complaint against those entrusted with the management of the Park; although it is not our first article on the subject. More than five years ago* we wrote and published an elaborate article entitled " Museums and Botanical Gardens," the design of which was to encourage those in charge of the Park at the time, and all who were in favor of making it worthy of our great city, by showing what had been accomplished in the chief capitals of the old world. We found no fault with any of the commissioners; not that we regarded their work as by any means faultless, but because, considering the disadvantages under which they labored, in laying, as it were, the foundation of the first great park in the United States, we thought they had acquitted themselves quite as well upon the whole as the most sanguine had a right to expect.

Perhaps it was their politics, some will say, that rendered them so worthy of our sympathy : but all who know us are aware that it is what a man is, and not what party he belongs to, we take into account. Whether a public functionary be a republican, a democrat, or a radical, does not influence us in the slightest degree in estimating his qualifications for the office he holds, or in forming an opinion of the use which he

* December, 1865, No. XXIII.

makes of such qualifications as he may happen to possess.
For aught we know, or care, the present commissioners are,
with one exception, of the same political creed as the former
commissioners. In common with all who glance at the news-
papers, we are, indeed, aware that Mr. Peter B. Sweeny belongs to the democratic party; we might as well pretend to be
ignorant of the existence of the illustrious James Fisk, Jr., or
of our equally illustrious quack doctors, as not to know, at
least, the avowed political dogmas of that distinguished person.

We are only sorry that he did not confine his attentions to
the party work he had been used to, and let our beautiful Park
alone. Had he done so it is by no means certain that his name
would ever have found its way into these pages. This is the
first time we have ever printed it, although made aware years
ago that Mr. Sweeny boasts of being the manager of the democratic party in New York, and one of our wealthiest politicians. Assuming both facts to be true, we confess we could
never understand how he became manager, or how he ac-
quired his wealth.

It is true we have seen him styled in the Herald "Peter *Bismarck* Sweeny"; but it should be known by this time
that no editor uses the figure of speech called irony in a style
more amusing, to those who can look beyond the surface of
things, than Mr. Bennett; nor is any one more fully aware that
nothing can render pygmies more ridiculous than to compare
them to giants. But let us assume that the countryman of
Burns and Smollett does not laugh in his sleeve when he uses
the term "Bismarck" in that sense, but does so in sober
earnest, which is assuming a good deal; nay, assuming that
there is some resemblance between the two personages, what
then? Be it remembered that it is not alone the faculty of
acting as the zealous, unscrupulous tool of the despot and
spoliator that Count Bismarck possesses in a high degree, for
he is equally cunning, greedy, and oblivious of principle in
smuggling the most stupid and good-for-nothing of his rela-
tives into positions where they also can fatten on the public

fodder, and become millionaires at the expense of the taxpayers.

If the term " Bismarck " is used as a sly allusion to this, then we admit that there is some force in it ; but we cannot help thinking that there would be much more force, and more justice, too, in comparing the present head (?) of the Department of Public Parks to his friend, Colonel Fisk, Jr. If the former claims to be a jurist, and the latter claims to be a military chieftain, we think that the legal attainments of the one are pretty nearly on a par with the military attainments of the other ; in other words, one is about as good a specimen of a field-officer as his friend is of a counsellor at law. We have no doubt that the latter could defend one for obtaining money under false pretences, or for conspiring with others for that purpose, as ably and fearlessly as the former could command a target company in charging a battalion of fishmongers before " the enemy " had time to arm.

By all means, then, let the middle name of our Park president be " Bismarck ;" we shall be entirely satisfied. We are bound to remember that other personages of somewhat similar calibre, as lawgivers and statesmen, have been elevated to a high pitch of glory by waggish writers. As an example, we need not go beyond the famous Sancho Panza. Cervantes is so anxious to do full justice to " honest Sancho," especially as the ruler of a certain island, that he prepares himself for the work as follows : " To thee I address myself, O sun ! by whose assistance man produces man ; thee I invoke to invigorate and enlighten my imagination, so that *my language may keep pace with its subject* and faithfully describe *the government of the great Sancho Panza.*"*

This it will be admitted is as full an " endorsement " of the pretensions of Sancho as ever Mr. Bennett has given of Sweeny And if the head of the latter has been turned by comparing him to his betters, so we are informed has been the head of the former.   But the subjects of Sancho required some qualifica-

---

* *Adventures of Don Quixote*, chap. xlv.

tions, however trifling, from those who aspired to rule them; for they address him thus : " It is an ancient custom here, my lord governor, that he who is appointed to the *command* of this far-famed island shall, on his first taking possession, give answer to some intricate and difficult questions, by which the people are enabled to judge of the capacity of their new governor, and thereby determine whether to rejoice or *grieve* at his arrival."*

We are informed that these people had heard compliments enough paid to Sancho ; as high compliments as ever have been paid to Sweeny. The chief difference seems to be that, while the inhabitants of the island of Barataria had the perception to distinguish the language of irony and derision from that of serious, sincere approbation, the inhabitants of the island of Manhattan—at least that portion of them that do most of the voting—take for gospel everything they are told, in an ingenious and lively manner.

This does not prove, however, that Mr. Sweeny is a fit and proper person to have the chief control of the Central Park. Had his rule been confined to the wild animals, then, with a few lessons from Barnum, he might have acquitted himself very well, and might in time have aspired, with some show of justice, to be styled Peter Barnum Sweeny. In the first place, we would not object to give him charge of the whole genus *vulpes*, although we understand that he is familiar with no nobler specimen of it than the *vulpes vulgaris*, so well known among henwives as the red fox. Nor should we fear that the genus *ursus*, especially the *ursus horribilis* (grizzly bear), would not receive appropriate treatment at his hands, or under his supervision. To these we should be willing to add the genus *sus*, including the *porcus Hibernicus*—as good a specimen of the domestic hog as we know ; and the genus *asinus*, including the *zebra Africana*, together with the whole family of the *simiadæ*, especially the baboon and green monkey species.

Some birds (*aves*) we would also place under his jurisdiction,

---

c *Adventures of Don Quixote*, chap. xlv.

although not those that could be plucked by throwing chaff in
their eyes, such as the *anseres Hibernici*, vulgarly called Irish
geese. This interesting but short-sighted species we should
rather keep out of his way ; but in their stead we would give
him some specimens of the genus *gallus*, which might include
the *gallina quæstura* (chamberlain's hen), a bird whose chief
characteristic, according to Pliny and other naturalists, is to set
up an enormous cackle, wonderfully similar to the braying of
the donkey, when her maw is so well filled that she can afford
to give a few small crumbs to the bantams and goslings at whose
expense she fattens ; whereas, while stuffing herself and her
greedy brood, she is as dumb as an owl at mid-day.

As for plants, we should trust none with Sweeny,
except very few of the hardier species, such as the genus
gabáisdhe,* the genus *práta*,† and the genus *tri-dhuile*.‡
These and a few others might receive proper treatment under
the rule of " President Sweeny ;" not indeed for love of the
people whose favored plants they are supposed to be, but for
love of their votes—that is, for love of the golden egg which,
hen or goose-like, he makes them lay for him and his friends.

But the question now is : How does Sweeny manage the
Central Park ? No intelligent person in the habit of visiting
it who makes any use of his eyes needs any reply to this.
But those who are shortsighted, as well as those who live too
far away to judge for themselves, may justly be told that
no Park involving half so much expense has ever been so
grossly mismanaged. We exaggerate nothing when we say
that an amount of damage has been done to the Park since
spring last, which it would take five years to remedy did the
work of the spoiler cease at this moment. We think we
hear our sagacious and accomplished naturalists exclaim,
with a derisive smile : " Why, he knows nothing about it !
he means the pruning, and thinning, and transplanting—what
nonsense ! " It is very true that we partly mean what you
designate by these terms ; it is also true that we believe in

---

° Irish for cabbage.   † Irish for potato.   ‡ Irish for shamrock.

pruning, thinning, and transplanting; but we believe in
them as we do in the use of the lancet, the scissors, and the
razor. Does it follow that, because these are useful instru-
ments in skilful, experienced hands, no mischief will be done
if almost anybody takes them up at random, and cuts and
hacks and mutilates whatever he imagines he can improve in
its health or appearance by his newly-acquired art ?

Most of our New York readers are aware that almost
immediately after Master Sweeny became president of the department of Public Parks he sailed for Europe. He visited
several parks in England and on the Continent, and, in
taking a hurried glance at each (for Tammany might go to
ruin if he was long absent), he observed that some little
branches had been lopped off here and there, a few trees
transplanted, and a few diseased ones cut down. It is said
that a word for the wise is sufficient; but Sweeny did not
require even a word. He returned as hastily as he went ; and
he was scarcely two days back in New York when he began
to prepare for a general onslaught on every grove, shrub-
bery, and tree in the Central Park ; his first attacks being
on those groups that had begun to afford a delightful shade—
one of the most fascinating attractions in a public park,
especially in a climate like ours, where everybody longs
for it in the summer, "as the hart panteth for the water
brooks.

Most persons have heard of the pet-monkey, which, having
observed the barber shaving his master, availed himself of the
first opportunity to steal the razor and lather-box, in order to
practise on the cat and dog, and such other members of the
family as he thought might be improved by the operation;
but Puss, Tray, etc., not relishing that sort of treatment, fought
to be let alone, or sought refuge in flight. In short, Master Simia
found that his friends did not care to be shaved; and whether in-
fluenced by undue enthusiasm in the exercise of his new
accomplishment, or by chagrin at the lack of appreciation for
his good intentions evinced by his friends, the poor animal

cut his own throat to such an extent that all the doctors in the neighborhood were unable to save his life.

If we learn nothing else from this little incident, it shows us the difference between animals and vegetables. Although the animal is "dumb," he is capable, in general, at least of seeking safety from his enemy in flight, whereas the tree must stand its ground and offer no resistance. Yet the tree, too, has life; it is capable of being wounded, and wounded fatally; *it is capable of contracting disease from bad, ignorant treatment; and the disease so contracted may, and often does, prove fatal.*

The most stupid might understand this, if aware that plants have a veritable circulation, and even respiration, corresponding with those of animals; and if Sweeny were aware of the important effects of those processes on our atmosphere, and consequently on the health of our citizens, we are willing to believe that even he would have paused before carrying the mutilating plan to the extreme extent he has.

We remarked at the beginning of this article, that we should not ask our readers to accept our views on the vitality and growth of plants any further than we might be found able to sustain them by the testimony of acknowledged authorities. First, we turn to "The Vegetable World" of Figuier, and find the two kingdoms compared as follows : "But the respiration of plants is not always the same like that of animals, in which carbonic acid gas, water, and vapor are exhaled without cessation either by day or night. Plants possess *two modes of respiration ;* one diurnal, in which the leaves absorb the carbonic acid of the air, *decompose this gas,* and extract the oxygen, while the carbon remains in their tissues; the other nocturnal, and *the reverse,* in which the plant absorbs the oxygen and extracts the carbonic acid; that is to say, *they breathe in the same manner that animals do.* The carbon which is used by plants during the day is indispensable to the perfect *development of their organs* and the consolidation of their tissues. *By respiration plants live and grow.*"*

---

* *The Veg. World :* Being a Hist. of Plants, with their Botanical Descriptions and Peculiar Properties, etc. By M. Louis Figuier, p. 198.

It is needless to remark to our readers, that by "plants" are meant trees and shrubs, as well as the common vegetables more popularly known by that name. But another word on this subject from M. Figuier : " The diurnal respiration of plants, which pours into the air considerable quantities of oxygen gas, happily compensates for the effects of animal respiration which produces carbonic gas injurious to the life of man. Plants *purify the air* injured by the respiration of men and animals. If animals transform the oxygen of the air into carbonic acid, *plants take this carbonic acid back again by their diurnal respiration.* They fix the carbon in the depth of their tissues, *and return oxygen to the air in respiration.*"[*]

Now, as to the circulation corresponding to the circulation of the blood in animals. This has been demonstrated in the clearest manner by numerous experiments. " If a plant is made to absorb colored liquid," says M. Figuier, " or if the *branches* are plunged into the same liquid, it is easily seen that it does not rise first *either in the bark or pith.* It is in the *wood* or *ligneous body* through which it manifestly takes its passage. This passage takes place through all the ligneous elements,—*cells, fibres, and vessels.* The *anatomical structure of these vessels,* their large number, their strength in the prostrate filiform and slender stems, which often attain a very considerable length, and which require to be traversed by a large quantity of sap in order to supply what is necessary for evaporation by the leaves—all these general facts *leave no doubt* as to the part which *the wood vessels* play in the *circulation of the sap.*"[†]

Referring to the curious and beatiful apparatus of Dr. Hales, an eminent English physiologist, by which these facts are illustrated, Figuier says : " Hales calculated from this that the force which impels the sap in the vine is *five times as great as that which impels the blood through the large arteries*

---

[*] *Ibid,* p. 109. See also Linnæus' *Systema Naturæ ; sive Regna Tria Naturæ.* Didot, Paris, 1830, pp. 75-80.—De Jussieu, *Genera Plantarum. Introduction,* p. 15 et seq.

[†] *Vegetable World,* p. 111.

of the horse. Having reached the leaves, the sap comes in contact with the air by the innumerable openings, or *stomates,* which communicate with the air cells and hollow *meatus* in the substance of the *parenchyma.*"*

This sap is just as necessary for the nourishment of the tree as the blood is for the nourishment of the animal; and, as whatever injures the blood, or its vessels, injures the animal, so whatever injures the sap, or its vessels, injures the tree. We do not say that the latter is in general as sensitive and tender as the former; but we maintain that one as well as the others sickens and dies from the treatment of ignorant quacks of the Sangrado type. Before we do anything more, however, than allude, in passing, to the indignation we have felt on different occasions, especially during the last three or four months, on seing dozens of common laborers mutilating the finest trees in the Park, while others stubbed up, or felled altogether, trees whose shade was becoming charming—so gratefully cool and refreshing when the heat is intolerable in every exposed place—we will briefly consider the subject in another light. Let us see what are the views of the best authorities on landscape gardening, and glance, if only for variety's sake, at the views of some of those regarded as the best judges of the beautiful in nature and art. First, we will turn to Loudon, who is the best English authority of the present day. Loudon is in favor of skilful pruning for certain kinds of trees; but for no trees would he allow the Sweeny style. Speaking of close pruning judiciously performed, he says :

" This mode of pruning is only adopted when the object is to produce stems or trunks clear of branches of any kind of protuberance, as in the case of standard trees in gardens, especially *fruit trees,* and in the case of forest trees *grown for their timber.* If the branch cut off *is under an inch in diameter,* the *wound* will generally *heal* over in two seasons, and *in this case* the timber sustains no practical injury ; *but if it is larger,* it will *probably begin to decay in the centre,*" etc.†

---

* *Vegetable World,* p. 112.   † Loudon's *Horticulture.*

Referring to the milder specimens of the Sweeny style, Loudon proceeds:

" Close lopping, by which *a large wound is produced*, the surface of which *not only never can unite with the new wood* which is formed over it, because, as we have seen, *growing tissue can only unite to growing tissue*, but the wood in the centre of *the wound* will, *in all probability*, begin *to rot* before it is covered over, and, consequently, the centre of the trunk *will be more or less injured*. Even if, by covering the wound with composition to exclude the weather, the surface of the section should be prevented from *rotting*, still there would be a blemish in the timber," etc.*

This, it will be admitted, is sufficiently clear ; it would enable any of our readers in the habit of visiting the Park to see whether our complaint is just or not. But we want to satisfy the most sceptical—we desire to convince even those who have the genius to make an empty sack stand, at least for a time, when they take it into their head. It is well known, by all who have travelled, that there are no better landscape gardeners at the present day than the Scotch. We have before us an excellent Scotch work, in several volumes, entitled " Rural Cyclopedia," and edited by the Rev. J. M. Wilson, of Edinburgh. From the article on pruning we extract the following :

" Where pruning is not required to renovate the vigor of *an enfeebled tree*, or to regulate its shape, in other words, in *the case of a healthy tree*, it may be considered *worse than useless.* * * *Ignorant cultivators* frequently *weaken the energies* of young trees, and cause them to grow up with lean and slender stems by injudiciously *pruning off* the young *side shoots*," etc.†

May we not ask, then, were all our fine trees at the Central Park " enfeebled " when its present head " cultivator " took charge of it ? Or must it be admitted that he is an " ignorant cultivator ? " But another word or two. Some may pretend that because Figuier, Loudon, and Wilson are men of our own day their authority may be questioned. In order that no such subterfuge can avail in this case, we will turn to old Evelyn, whose *Silva et Terra* has the classic

---

Loudon's *Horticulture*, p. 340.   † *Rur. Cyc.*, Edinburgh, 1852.

stamp, and who has elicited the praises of the greatest modern naturalists, including Buffon and Cuvier, especially for his admirable dissertations on the treatment of trees in public parks and gardens. He, also, is in favor of judicious pruning in those instances in which pruning seems to be required ; but that he has as great a horror as we have ourselves of the Sweeny style, may be inferred from the following :

" It is a misery to see how *our fairest trees are defaced and mangled by unskilful woodmen* and mischievous borderers, who go always armed with short hand-bills, *hacking and chopping off all that comes in their way ;* by which our trees are made full of *knots, stubs, boils, cankers, and deformed branches to their utter destruction.*"*

That " unskilful woodmen " are unsafe persons to entrust with the care of a public park or garden, will be readily admitted ; but they can hardly be said to be more unsafe in that position than a ward politician, even though the latter may be led by satirically-inclined friends, amused by his vanity, to fancy himself a statesman and lawgiver. Be this as it may, we ask the reader to notice how " our fairest trees are defaced and mangled," and how they are " made full of knots, stubs, boils, and cankers, etc., to their utter destruction." A little further on in the same page Evelyn laments that those ignorant people " have no consideration how those *ghastly wounds mortally affect the whole body of the tree,*" etc. And that Evelyn understood vegetable physiology as well as landscape gardening, is sufficiently proved by the reasons which he assigns for the " boils, cankers," etc. " It is," he says, " abundantly evident that *all trees inspire and expire, from pores in their bark as well as their leaves, so that whatever interrupts either of those processes must occasion disease.*"†

Now we venture to say that no impartial reader, aware of what has been done of late at the Park, who has accompanied us thus far, will think that we have deviated from the language of moderation and justice in asserting, at the beginning

---

* Evelyn's *Silva et Terra,* vol. ii. p. 173.

† *Silva et Terra,* edited by Hunter, vol. ii. p. 182.

of this paper, that more mischief has been done to the trees
under Sweeny rule during the last six months than can be
remedied in as many years. We now add, in the same calm
but earnest spirit, that he should be restrained from pursu-
ing his ignorant and destructive course any further. The
British parliament has, at different times, enacted laws
for the purpose of restraining "ignorant or ill-disposed
persons." Besides the well-known statutes 1 George I. and
6 George III., there is still on the statute book of England
what is called the Black Act, by which, " to cut down or destroy any trees planted in an avenue, or growing in a garden, orchard, *or plantation for ornament*, shelter, or profit, is
*felony without benefit of clergy; and the hundred shall be charg-
able for the damages unless the offender be convicted."* The
Sixth of George III. made the penalty for the same offence
transportation for seven years. These laws make no allow-
ance for ignorance or presumption ; and if those whose duty it
was to restrain the offender failed to do so, either because he
was a political ring-leader, or for any other motive, they had
to pay, themselves, for the damage he had done.

We shall not pause now to inquire what might be the effect
of such a law in the present case ; but referring to the Black
Act reminds us of an incident which may serve as an episode.
As we rode along one day, not far from the Ramble, we observed about a dozen persons, all armed with weapons more
or less formidable, with which they were making an onslaught
on a beautiful group of trees, as if their object had been to
provide themselves with fire-wood, or with roofing for their
shanties, without any regard to consequences. Approaching
within a dozen yards or so, we addressed the nearest in as
good-humored a tone as the nature of the work going forward
would allow us: "May I ask what are you destroying the
trees for ?" There was a pause for a moment. The men
looked at each other, and after a moment one replied with an
expressive grin, " Faith, an' it is that same, sir ; but 'tis n't
our fault. It's th' ordhers of Misther Swiny himself." " Mis-

ther Sweeny, the prasident, you mane," interrupted another, drawing his pipe somewhat abruptly from his mouth. Before we had time to reply in the affirmative a third person, armed with a weapon like a scythe, laughed, and said in Irish, "*Tha thissa karth a Vichael; a ainm fior bu Swiny.*" (You are right, Michael; his true name *was Swiny.*) Another, equally disposed to joke, said, in the same dialect, "*Shay shid ainm Sassenach; a ainm fior shay Mac Finsigh.*" (But that's his English name; his true name is ——.) Here there was a general laugh; but we prefer not to translate "Mac Finsigh" for the present. "It isn't Mr. Sweeny's name I want to inquire about, but what you are doing to the trees." "If it was, thin," says another, "'twouldn't be Misther Sweeny, savin' your presence, but Misther Beesmark Sweeny." "By jabers, Barney, isn't ould Bennett capital at makin' *omadhanes* (fools) of those polititioners wid his dhroll names." "But what of the trees, Mike?" "Well, in ould Ireland the threes wouldn't stand this sort o' prunin', but in the land o' liberty may be 't will be good for them! I'll hould a bet wid any body, that's the *iday!* for did n't Misther Swiny go all the way to Dublin, the moment he was promoted, to see the threes in the Finix Park and the Boar de Bulone, and all them other cilibrated places?" Despairing of receiving any more satisfactory information in that quarter, we thanked Mike, Larry, and Barney, and proceeded to enjoy our ride in the best way we could.*

---

* Revolving in our mind some of the expressions in the Irish language we had just heard, it occurred to us that Barney knew something about etymology, although there was no evidence that he had ever studied either that or any other branch of learning. On a little reflection we remembered that neither of the letters *w* and *y*, which occur in the name Sweeny, belong to the Erse language, and that the original Irish of Sweeny is *Suibine* with the prefix Mac (*son of*),which is identical with the Latin *Suidæ*, the name of a family which, though very ancient and highly interesting in some of its characteristics, is held in abhorence alike by Jew and Mohammetan. (Vide Molloy's Grammar of the Irish Language, p. 214.) Happening to see a good deal of rooting just at the moment, and bearing in mind some of the more salient points of Darwin's theory of natural selection in the struggle for life, we had a great mind to return and thank Barney for so curious a lesson in comparative philology, especially as he could possibly tell us why the prefix " Mac" has been omitted in the case of " the prasident;" but lest we might come in contact, by mistake, with some of the " pruning hooks," we thought it best to pursue our researches in some other direction.

Now, leaving the reader to judge for himself as to the amount of injury done to the trees, we proceed to consider what is the effect of the lopping, hacking, stubbing, and felling system on the scenery; and whether shade is to be regarded as essential to the attractiveness of a public park, or the reverse. That nature may be improved by art is admitted by all who have any taste; but the art must not be apparent. The eye must not be offended by the rents and tears of weapons; nature must be kept in mind, and, to use the language of Linnæus, *Natura non facit saltus.* In his essay on the Sublime and Beautiful, Burke very justly says: "No work of art can be great but as it deceives; to be otherwise is the prerogative of nature only."* He was not a mere politician and trickster who has given this opinion, but a statesman and a philosopher. And Walpole, writing in the same spirit, tells us that under the supervision of the intelligent superintendent, who had some knowledge of botany, " The living landscape was *chastened or polished, not transformed. Freedom was given to the forms of trees; they extended their branches unrestricted,*" etc.

But we need not have consulted any more recent or better authority as to the proper care of trees, or what constitutes a beautiful park or garden, than the author of the Æneid; for there is no finer essay on horticulture and landscape gardening in any language than the second Georgic of Virgil. Accordingly it is extensively quoted by the best modern writers on those subjects, including the great Linnæus himself. As for Evelyn, his *Sylva* contains extracts at almost every page from this truly scientific and admirable poem. But it is not alone in his second Georgic that the Mantuan bard celebrates the cool and grateful shade as one of the greatest blessings which the inhabitants of a populous city can enjoy; in the very first line presented to us of his poems he makes Melibœus sing:

---

* Part II. sec. 10.

Tityre, tu patulæ recubans *sub tegmine fagi*
Sylvestrem tenui Musam meditaris avena.*

Before proceeding further than the fourth line he presents
the delightful idea in another form—

Tu, Tityre, *lentus in umbra*
Formosam resonare doces Amaryllida *sylvas*.†

To extract what is appropriate and instructive in the
second Georgic were to extract nearly the whole poem. But
a line or two will suffice. First, the poet reminds the horti-
culturist that nature is various in producing trees—

Principio arboribus varia natura creandis.‡

Virgil also warns the ignorant pruner (*putator*) by re-
minding him that the branches of one tree may turn into
another without injury to either—

Et sæpe alterius *ramos impune videmus*
Vertere in alterius.§

Nor does the poet forget to show that trees, like animals,
should be treated according to their different kinds and con-
stitutions—not treated all alike after our Sangrado fashion—

Quare agite proprios generatim discite cultus.‖

Thus Virgil not only expresses the highest admiration for
the shady recesses of the groves as a feature of the landscape grateful to all, but he shows how those recesses may be
produced. Still greater, if possible, is the admiration of
Horace for the delightful gloom formed by the intertwining
trees with their luxuriant foliage. As an illustration of this,
we need only refer to his description of his own villa on the
banks of the Tiber, the munificent gift of Mæcenas. It
charms him to see the vine and the elm embrace each other
so closely as to exclude the burning rays of the sun (an
amicta vitibus ulmo); it delights him to proclaim that the
breezy hills are separated only by umbrageous valleys.

---

* O Tityrus, recumbent beneath the shade of a spreading beech, etc.—
Bucolica, Ecl. 1.

† O Tityrus, while reposing in the shade, teach the trees to resound
the name of the fair Amaryllis.

‡ V. 9.   § V. 32, 33.   ‖ V. 35.

Contenui montes, nisi dissocientur opaca
Valle.*

Cicero, Varro, and Pliny evince equal admiration for the
spreading branches, and equal indignation against the spoiler
who would lop them off and banish the Dryades with the
shades they love. But neither poet, nor botanist, nor horti-
culturist, ancient or modern, has more eloquently, or more
plainly shown what a public garden or park ought to be than
Milton. He delights to recur again and again in several
books of his Paradise Lost to the scenery of the garden of
Eden ; accordingly, the chief landscape gardeners of France,
Germany, and Italy, as well as England, who have treated the
subject since his time, have quoted him as an authority on
those subjects. The great English poet delights to tell that
even Satan pauses in his diabolical course when he reaches
the border where the delicious Garden

> " Crowns with her enclosure green,
> As with a *rural mound* the champain head
> Of a deep wilderness, whose *hairy sides*
> *With thicket overgrown, grotesque and wild,*
> *Access denied ;* and overhead up grew
> Insuperable height *of loftiest shade*
> Cedar, and pine and fir and branching palm,
> A sylvan scene ; and, as the ranks ascend
> *Shade above shade, a woody theatre*
> *Of stateliest view.†*

Even the " sapphire fount," the " crisped brooks," the
" orient pearl," and " sands of gold," are all enhanced in their
beauty by being viewed " under pendant shades." Then we
are told about the plants and flowers

> " Which *not nice art*
> In beds and *curious knots*, but *nature boon*
> Pour'd forth *profuse* on hill, and dale, and plain
> Both where the morning sun first warmly smote
> The open field, and where *the unpierced shade*
> *Imbrowned the noon-tide bowers.*"‡

○ Epist., xvi., Ad Quinctium, lib. 1.
† *Par. Lost*, B. iv. v. 133 et seq.   ‡ *Ibid*, v. 241 et seq.

It is well known that Milton had made himself acquainted, as far as he could do so by careful study and research, with the most charming features of all the famous gardens both of the ancient and modern world, before he wrote a line of his description of Eden. To him the sacred grove of Diana, the garden of Epicurus, the paradise of Persia, the suspended gardens of Babylon, the Villa Adriana, the floating gardens of Mexico, and the villas of Netzahualoyotl and Montezuma, were equally familiar. But it will be seen that to no features essential to a park or garden does the great poet—whose ideas of the beauties of nature and art are universally and justly admired—attach more importance than to " the thicket overgrown," though " grotesque and wild," " the unpierced shade," and " noon-tide bowers."* These are the beauties which would cause even the arch-enemy of man to pause before he attempted to destroy them, but whose destruction, as far as it is in his power, is the first care of Mr. Peter B. Sweeny.

Several generations ago, from the time of Walpole to that of Pope and Addison, the English had to complain as we have now ; still more recently, Mr. Knight has very spiritedly and justly protested against

> " Each secret haunt and deep recess *display'd*
> And intricacy *banished with its shade.*"

Nor does he conceal his indignation against the ignorant spoiler, whom he addresses as follows :

> " Hence, hence ! thou *haggard fiend, however called,*
> Thou meagre genius of the bare and bald ;
> Thy spade and mattock here at length lay down
> And follow to the tomb your favorite Brown."†

Had our leading papers so addressed our Brown two or three months since, much mischief might have been prevented. We are convinced that had their principal editors been in the habit of visiting the Park regularly, they would have done so. Surely

---

* See also v. 291, vii. 527, viii. 304, ix. 439.
‡ *Landscape*, p. 25, ed. 2.

the veteran who contributed at least as much as any one else to
establish the Central Park, would not have looked on in silence
had he been aware of the treatment it has been receiving under
the Sweeny rule ; we are sure that " Bismarck " would have
given way to the much more appropriate name of Breun, or
Brofy, Bradly, Bradach,* Bunkum, etc., etc. Poor Mr. Ray-
mond, who used to visit the Park almost daily, and take great
delight in observing the luxurious growth of the trees—we can
well imagine how indignant he would have felt ; for he, too,
was entitled to a full share of the glory of securing for New
York so priceless a boon. Has the Times become indifferent
to what was so dear to its able and worthy founder ? Can
nothing excite the indignation of our other leading daily editors
but partisan politics ? Has Mr. Greeley no protest to make,
even as an agriculturist, against a more deplorable exhibition
than the bull in the china shop, and the bear, too—the veritable *ursus horribilis ?* Must the World remain dumb because,
although aware that it is evidently as absurd, if not as cruel,
to entrust Sweeny with the care of the trees and shrubs at
the Central Park, as it would be to entrust the wolf with
the care of the sheep and lambs, still it is bound to remember
that that personage is a very smart fellow at election time,
when he boasts that in spite of press or pulpit he carries the
Irish vote in his pocket ? We would fain hope not ; and yet
the work of destruction still goes on. No one has less
excuse than the Express, for few visit the Park more frequently than Mr. Brooks and his handsome cream-colored
ponies. He and Mr. Hastings would be much better occupied in exclaiming " Ringman, spare that tree ! " than in
going to law with each other ; especially as the latter under-
stands Irish ethnology, including the interesting tribes of
the *suidæ* and *simiadæ,* better than most other American
editors, and ought to understand the dialects of both the
mixed and pure breeds. As to the Post, we fear it is too
busily occupied in eulogising all books and pamphlets bearing

---

* Vide Foley's *Irish Dictionary.* Dublin. Curry & Co. 1855.

the imprint of wealthy publishers, and watching the seething of
the political caldron to see what will turn up, to find time to
bestow any attention on such abstract subjects as horticulture
and botany. At all events, we are not sure but that its managers
regard the transformations recently undergone by the Park
as equal to certain recent translations which are said to surpass
all others ever made. Then our little luminary no longer
shines in that direction; it seems that, unlike the orb from which
it borrows its name, it has its dark side, which it occasionally
uses as a cloak for its new friends. Hence it is, we suppose, that
what was all *blubber* only a few months ago is now all "Brains;"
a phenomenon which reminds us of a certain learned professor
who spent half his life in denouncing *pork* as a very unwhole-
some and rather disgusting sort of food, but suddenly discov-
ered, in some mysterious way, that, after all, it was just the
thing—better than beef or mutton—especially for persons of
delicate constitution supposed to have the scrofulous taint.
True, the pork was pork still, and nobody but our philosopher
could see that its essential properties had undergone any
change.

That our Tammany naturalist has done some good, however,
far be it from us to deny. If his wish in doing it was only to
oblige two or three of his worthy friends, what of that? It
is proper to say, however, that in speaking of his "friends"
we do not mean those said to belong to "the ring." As we
know nothing very overbearing, arrogant, or pompous of the
latter, there is no reason why we, who have nothing to do with
partisan politics, should treat them as if we knew the reverse.
Thus, for example, we have never known Mr. Connolly to
make any offensive or parvenu-like display in the Park or
elsewhere; on the contrary, we have always known him to
take his drive as quietly and unobtrusively, though as spiritedly, as any private gentleman. If Mr. Tweed has pursued
any different course—if he has exhibited the least ostentation
that any one should take umbrage at—we have never wit-
nessed, or been made aware of, the fact. As for Mr. Brennan

no one avails himself of the advantages of the Park more modestly than he, with his plain one-horse wagon and his bow and smile, in passing, for rich and poor alike.   If, with this experience, we should seek to cast slurs on those gentlemen, merely because they are public functionaries, or because their political opinions differ from ours, we should reproach ourselves as unfair and unjust.

But everybody in the habit of visiting the Park during the last six months is aware that " Cononel" Fisk and " Dr." Helmbold have experienced considerable difficulty in showing off their coaches-and-six on that part of the eastern drive extending from Eighty-sixth to a Hundred and second street. That citizens so illustrious, and to whom the public owe so much, as the Erie Cononel and the Buchu Doctor should be unable to turn their equipages in any part of the road, so that they could drive up and down as often as they thought necessary for a full exhibition, without running the risk of coming in contact with vulgar one-horse, or, at most, two-horse people, was a hardship which, of course, " Brains " Sweeny was not slow to recognize.   We are not aware whether the " doctor " is, or has been, a colleague of his, like the " colonel "; however, be this as it may, it is but fair to take into account that it is exactly the same class, i.e., the most ignorant and most credulous, who do the voting for Sweeny and buy the buchu for Helmbold.   Ignorance and imbecility are as much the basis of the greatness of the one as they are that of the greatness of the other.   Besides, as one cures all trees and shrubs, Sangrado like, by lopping off their best branches, or felling them altogether, so does the other cure all men and women, let their maladies be what they may, by dosing them with buchu ; and we all know that a fellow-feeling makes one wondrous kind. Accordingly the decree has gone out, and in due time there will be room enough for Fisk and Helmbold.   Let no one complain, when the bills are sent in, that it is dear work, for it will be very cheap compared to the " pruning."   Supposing the work of destroying each tree costs $10 (which, it must be ad-

mitted, is a moderate estimate), without any regard to the consequences of that destruction, and that the widening of the road
costs the same amount per square foot, should we not remember that it is better to pay even an exorbitant price for what
is useful and good, than to pay any price for what is injurious
and destructive ?